Little Inventions

PIZZA

RAPHAËL FEJTÖ

FIREFLY BOOKS

The history of pizza is ancient. A long time ago, people loved eating different types of pancakes. To make them, flour and water were mixed together and then made into a ball.

The dough was flattened.

Then put in the stone oven
to cook until crisp.

Salt and aromatic herbs, such as rosemary and garlic, were added to the pancakes to make them taste better.

Since they were cheap and delicious, everyone ate them. It was even the soldiers' main meal.

One day, in the 16th century, a merchant went on a trip to America and came back to Naples in Italy, with something incredible. It was completely red, and round. It was... a tomato!

But, since people worried that the tomatoes were poisonous, nobody wanted to try them. Scientists studied them in order to understand what they could be used for.

Finally, so as to not take any risks, it was decided they would be used as decorations, like flowers.

For a long time, nobody in Italy ate tomatoes. However, one day, a cook from Naples who had a desire to invent new recipes, had the idea to cook tomatoes and pour the juice on the pancake.

He was very excited, but also a little scared. What if the tomatoes actually were poisonous?

He looked for volunteers to taste his invention, but nobody would. So he decided to try it himself. He thought it was delicious and he didn't even get sick!

Soon everybody in Naples wanted to taste this new dish. The cook, who they called *pizzaiolo*, (pizza-maker) made lots of them.

The *pizzaiolo* was very organized: he prepared the pizza and as soon as it was ready, his assistant carried it on his head on an iron plate and ran through the streets of the city singing, to announce its arrival.

The Neapolitans, foodies that they were, bought slices after work, and ate them quickly on their way back home.

Eventually, people loved the pizzas so much
they came to get them right out of the oven.

The *pizzaiolo* had the idea to open a little counter where he could sell his pizzas.

Then he suggested that people eat them on the spot.

YUM!

He made pizzas with sausage, ham, vegetables, or just tomato.

There was something for everyone.

Eventually, pizza become so popular even poets praised this delicious dish in their poems...

... and musicians composed songs.

Pizza was the dish that brought people together, the rich and the poor. It became the symbol and the pride of southern Italy.

One day, the queen of Italy insisted that she taste this new dish everyone was talking about. She ordered one from the best *pizzaiolo* of Naples: Raffaele Esposito.

To honor his queen, Raffaele decided to make a new pizza with the colors of the Italian flag. He used tomato for red, basil for green, and finally, for white, he used melted mozzarella, a delicious Italian cheese.

The queen invited all her friends to
discover the mysterious pizza.

But the noblemen were very upset
that the queen was serving them a
commoners' dish.

The queen decided to taste it, and when she saw the melted cheese running everywhere, she almost ordered her guard to throw the *pizzaiolo* in prison.

But once she ate her first bite… she loved
the pizza so much she sent a letter to thank
Raffaele with all her heart.

*Dear Raffaele, this was the
best thing I've ever eaten in my
entire life, thank you so much!
Margherita.

Of course, Raffaele became the proudest *pizzaiolo* in Naples. He decided to call his specialty the "Margherita" pizza in honor of his queen.

Even today, when you go into a pizzeria, you can order a Margherita pizza and it will still be the same as Raffaele's, the best *pizzaiolo* in the whole world!

And you, what's your favorite

?

There you go, now you know everything
about the invention of the PIZZA!

But do you remember
everything you've read?

Play the MEMORY game to see
what you remember!

MEMORY GAME

1. What were tomatoes used for before they were eaten?

2. In which country was pizza invented?

3. What do you call the chef who makes pizzas?

4. What is the name of the queen for whom Raffaele Esposito made a pizza?

5. What are the colors of the Italian flag?

1. They were used as decorations.
2. Italy.
3. The pizzaiolo.
4. Margherita.
5. Green-White-Red.

31

A FIREFLY BOOK

Published by Firefly Books Ltd. 2016

Source edition © 2015 Le Pizza, ÉDITIONS PLAY BAC, 33 rue du Petit-Musc, 75004, Paris, France, 2015

This translated edition copyright © 2016 Firefly Books

First printing

Publisher Cataloging-in-Publication Data (U.S.)

Names: Fejtö, Raphaël, author. | Greenspoon, Golda, translator. | Mersereau, Claudine, translator.
Title: Pizza / Raphaël Fejtö.
Description: Richmond Hill, Ontario, Canada : Firefly Books, 2016. | Series: Little Inventions | Originally published by Éditions Play Bac, Paris, 2015 as Les p'tites inventions: La Pizza | Summary: "This brief history on one of the small, overlooked inventions we use in our everyday lives, in a six-part series is geared toward children. With fun and quirky illustrations and dialog, it also comes with a memory quiz to ensure children retain what they learn" -
- Provided by publisher.
Identifiers: ISBN 978-1-77085-749-0 (hardcover)
Subjects: LCSH: Pizza – History -- Juvenile literature.
Classification: LCC TX770.P58F458 |DDC 641.8248 – dc23

Library and Archives Canada Cataloguing in Publication

Fejtö, Raphaël
[Pizza. English]
        Pizza / Raphaël Fejtö.
(Little inventions)
Translation of: La pizza.
ISBN 978-1-77085-749-0 (bound)
        1. Pizza--History--Juvenile literature. I. Title.
II. Title: Pizza. English.
TX770.P58F4613 2016   j641.82'48   C2016-900072-9

Published in the United States by
Firefly Books (U.S.) Inc.
P.O. Box 1338, Ellicott Station
Buffalo, New York 14205

Published in Canada by
Firefly Books Ltd.
50 Staples Avenue, Unit 1
Richmond Hill, Ontario L4B 0A7

Printed in China

playBac

les p'tites inventi